GW00374518

AWAKEN

To Angela,
May Love, Light and
laughter always walk
with you.
May truth ever
be your guide

Always Richard.

Copyright © 2007 R R Ritchie

The moral right of the author has been asserted.

Apart from any fair dealing for the purposes of research or private study,
or criticism or review, as permitted under the Copyright, Designs and Patents
Act 1988, this publication may only be reproduced, stored or transmitted, in
any form or by any means, with the prior permission in writing of the
publishers, or in the case of reprographic reproduction in accordance with
the terms of licences issued by the Copyright Licensing Agency. Enquiries
concerning reproduction outside those terms should be sent to the publishers.

Matador
9 De Montfort Mews
Leicester LE1 7FW, UK
Tel: (+44) 116 255 9311 / 9312
Email: books@troubador.co.uk
Web: www.troubador.co.uk/matador

ISBN: 978-1905886-982

The author can be contacted at
richard.reid999@btinternet.com
07961 025336

Matador is an imprint of Troubador Publishing Ltd

In Memory of Ann Brocklebank.

...A true earth angel.

AWAKEN

**Inspirational writing, words and wisdom
Encompassing evil, evolution
and
enlightenment.**

By

R. R. Ritchie.

'The Lisan'

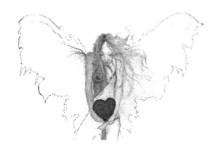

ACKNOWLEDGEMENTS

AND DEDICATION

This book is before you now only through the belief, encouragement, praise, wishes and often, well aimed physical, and/or verbal boot up the backside of so many others.

Another book would be required to list them all separately as I have been blessed in life with the company and acquaintance of wonderful people.

Each and everyone of them adding their own personal contribution in a multitude of ways, including those generous strangers whose reactions and comments allowed me to understand the effect of my words on other's and therefore, develop faith in its worth.

Those closest to me need no further evidence of my deep and lasting gratitude. You know who you are, and you also know how loved and important to me you have been and remain. Thank you for being my family, friends and support.

I dedicate this book to, through, and with as much love as I have managed to embrace, to all the above, but especially to my beautiful and very talented daughter Dawn, who drew the breathtaking and inspirational work of art that became our logo known as "THE ANGEL of the DAWN". So often, while on display or sale to the public, it has been this that has captured the eye and drawn people to read the words that the 'angel' adorns.

This book cannot be dedicated to the one person who above and beyond any doubt deserves it most. She has with love, determination, strength of will and self-sacrifice, striven and driven to bring my work into the public domain. Solely through her dedication, belief and endless hard work an enterprise known as 'The Lisan' was born. With wonderful flair, imagination, skill and creativity, she combined my words, Dawn's, and other images, with crystal and feather to produce fabulous framed, exquisite examples of our work for public appreciation. She has now begun to add even more by writing beautiful insightful and inspired words of her own.
To our great delight our work is now in homes throughout the globe where it has found an appreciative and generously complementary audience.
There would be none of this without her, she was and is the driving force and true spirit of the "Lisan"
She is my helpmate, share-mate and soul mate. I cannot dedicate this book to the one who deserves it most because, in truth, Katrina, this is...YOUR BOOK.
Always Light, Always Love, Always thank you
Richard.

FOREWORD

This is a mind map, a journey from the external, through the internal, and on into the eternal.

Humanity hovers in a miniscule molecule it calls reality declaring it complete, while within us, our awareness whispers of a wider wisdom, a deeper understanding.

We are taught how to feel, think, behave, react and respond, from the womb. Through infancy, childhood, teenage, and also in adulthood, it is another persons image of life that we adopt, and so often, never question, that teaches experience, expertise, ability, competence or skill. Those imprinted programmes we carry throughout our lifetimes believing them to be our own ideas and ideals. Programmed people pursuing programmed purposes in a packaged personality we believe to be our own. Parents, environment, culture and creed, condition us into complete compliance. This is not done meaningfully, they simply follow the conditioning code that they also were imprinted with, then, just like a virulent computer virus, it is passed on. Not many individuals take the time to scan their own personal 'Main Driver' so never discover the 'Trojan Horse' within. Of those who do, the seeming complexity of the 'man machine' is enough to make them believe it is beyond their skill to fix, 'and anyway it works as well as most', is enough of an excuse to continue working with a faulty Framework.

From this confused consciousness we develop fear. Fear of not getting it right, of doing it wrong, of being different, of being the same, of being to blame, of not fitting in, of not standing out, etc., etc.

Fear rules us and entraps us in a web of self-deceit, gluing us to our front row seat in the film-theatre of fake feeling. It is this fear that prevents us from peeling back the persona skins suffocating our true self and discovering the marvel of ME. Constantly, we judge ourselves through another's eyes or by another's values, while our souls scream in silence.

Here an attempt is made to put that screaming silence into harmonious speech, wisdom into words, an essay of emotions, a lesson in learning through the language of love.

Science has of late been rocked by quantum physics bringing into question the very foundations from which it drew its conclusions and on which much of it's basic beliefs are based. So called facts now falter and fail under the atomic microscope, and the courage of those who questioned the creed and culture that conditioned and controlled through finance and fear.

Greed and egotism have governed mankind. These have been the paradigms of our past and present. Now, there is a universal 'AWAKENING'!!!

Soul, and science should never have been split asunder. The cosmos calls with the identical rhythm that throbs in the core of our D.N.A., we hum in harmony with the heavens, our soul sense sings the song of the celestial sky. We now know how little is known. The life we are living is the illusion, we need to learn our lesson and live in love.

This book is written from personal observation, experience and occasional insight, no judgements are made or are necessary. Find within that which comforts, inspires, aids or enlightens, but please find a sharing within these words. We are never alone only afraid of being so.

R.R.Ritchie
In love

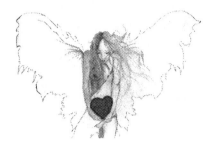

INTRODUCTION

Within these pages all aspects of life are examined through personal
experience, contact and observation.

Having been written with and in, honesty, pain, laughter and love. Take what you wish from the words included here, or, reject them if you so desire.
It has been divided into three sections :- 'LIFE'…
'LEARNING'… 'LIGHT and LOVE.'
Understanding can only be achieved through complete comprehension of the context in which anything is said, written or experienced, which is the reason for opening the book with a small selection of theorems including 'Understanding...Understanding'.
Where possible I have placed the pieces in the categories I feel most appropriate, although, some may be equally suited to another category or indeed all three. I leave the final choice up to you.

'LIFE' deals with that which is encountered through and from interaction with others and the programmes which this engenders in us.

'LEARNING' encourages the growth of self examination a questioning mind encounters.

'LIGHT and LOVE' is the step towards the soul sense. That which inspires, creates and causes spiritual maturity.

May you find comfort, hope, inspiration, joy, meaning and love within these pages.
May you find a reflection and a sharing in my words.
But most of all. May you find YOU!!!

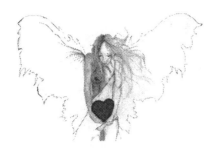

CONTENTS

Theorems

LIFE

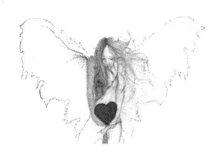

LEARNING

LOVE and LIGHT

PROPHECIES

Theorems

Rest in Peace: -

Rest in Peace: -
  So much has been said and written, about the positive power, beauty, and inner peace of solitude. Of going within oneself, into the silence, the contemplation of the id and reaching that blissful state of self-awareness, then self-love There is truth in this path, yet - only a step towards "The Truth". If god has truly set in each of us a divine spark, what purpose does aspiring towards that spark serve?

Enlightenment may well come with solitude, inner tranquillity and quiet meditation; but to find one's true nature, there must be honesty and balance. That balance can surely only come with knowledge, wisdom and perception, gained through and during interaction with others, and understanding the causes that influence or induce: - happiness, discontent, anger, jealousy etc, in them. Thus allowing us to identify the same emotions in ourselves. How these emotions are displayed also allows us to recognise the same faults, traits and failings underlying our own, often-poor behaviour. In so doing they should inspire us to strive towards a higher awareness of the true motivations,- mental, physical and spiritual, behind our own actions, re-actions, and human nature. People are the mirror through which we can truly view ourselves.

Understanding brings realization of what is base in our nature, and with this understanding, what is great and good. With this comes the "desire to aspire".

Honesty, is knowing we deceive ourselves, knowledge comes with this honesty,

Wisdom is using this knowledge to improve oneself.

Always I hear of the individual and read of this inner peace, this state of inner harmony being the great goal of the true individual. To learn to be in love with oneself is supposedly to learn to be at peace with oneself. Is this the peak of human perfection and harmony?

Once, I walked this path of peace, at one (I thought), with nature, God and myself. Therein lies the paradox, sole, alone, solitary and myself, calm, serene, tranquil, and isolated. At peace?... many gravestones bear that epitaph, "Rest in peace"!

But surely only after much effort and soul searching is there a time to enjoy this newfound tranquillity. Wisdom has lead you to this state of self-satisfaction and now... wisdom should lead you logically, emotionally and spiritually onto the next inevitable step.

Be it God, your higher self, or whatever force you believe in that has brought you to this point, now is the time to reason why? What purpose does being content with oneself serve other than self-satisfaction... none! Its true purpose is to awaken the counter balance, the love of life within.

It is wonderful to walk in joy and recognition of all the beauty surrounding us, a raindrop on a leaf, a storm lashed shore, the sky, wind, earth and all the marvels of nature. This recognition allows us to remain apart in the midst of the mayhem of modern man, to walk with peace while others madly race to achieve more meaningless material means...to know how futile their search for outward contentment is. But, therein once again lies the paradox of this teaching of self-awareness, self-knowledge, and self-content...it's all to do with self!

19

Individuals are things apart, by definition, they have no need, use, wish, want, desire or incentive, to interact with anything or anyone else.
To be totally independent means being self-sufficient, self-sustaining, self-absorbed, self-reliant, and therefore,... self-opinionated. Content with the self, sure of the self and sure therefore that self-opinion is right. This means that there is no room, or need for any other opinions. This is arrogance, and arrogance leads not to wisdom but to blindness and bigotry. The correct term would be... selfish!
In all life there is a circle of learning.
The fool, (of hermetic lore) begins his journey and passes through all stages and states of enlightenment, finally arriving back at his journey's start. Now however, he knows exactly what makes him a fool and in this knowledge is his wisdom, truth and freedom.
All esoteric teaching has at its core this awareness of contradiction, contrast and counterbalance. For example...truth within truth, understanding beyond understanding, the question formed by the answer, wisdom within why. The further sight, the further step.
In so many of the self-realisation and self-empowerment teachings, the sole aim is to be self-sufficient, self-reliant, self-loving and self absorbed. Without a true heart and/or truly enlightened guidance, this can so
easily result in the delights of delusion. The ideology of the id is neither innocence nor ignorance misled into imagined illumination. That is where the ego eats, also known as "narcissism", the fool returned but now an arrogant fool. No desire, wisdom, or wish to enlighten himself further,

20

content in his complacency, his inner peace an insular shell, his calmness... corruption.

How wonderful to share, to share your love of all things with another, to share your knowledge, wisdom, peace, tranquillity, joy and contentment. To touch the God spark within you, then... reach out and touch that same God spark in another. To form a union with God within yourself and a union with God in others.

All who proclaim to be at peace with themselves and state they have reached "Nirvana", still seem to suffer from the urge, need, and impulse, to tell others of this wonderful condition. Why?... again, the paradox!

If indeed they had found this total inner contentment, that total oneness with self and the universe, there would be no need or wish to speak, write or inform others. Contentment would be constant. Why would they still wish, want, feel impelled or desire to impart their wisdom to others?

Surely that same wisdom should have taught...to bring others into their surroundings, in an attempt to enlighten them, must and will bring them into contact with a higher and lower level of perception than their own? This will therefore need constant adjustment in adapting to individual needs, understanding each particular level of perception a person has attained of their teaching. They are no longer alone, at peace, tranquil. Interaction with them, their emotions, life's, expectations, dreams, hopes, desires must disturb this inner tranquillity. Even if only in their ability to empathise with others emotional struggles to comprehend or dispute their assertions.

Loving oneself, must, through logic, lead you to the capability to love others. To truly love another, you share all their emotions and therefore share their sadness, fear, desire, dreams and disappointments. To truly share with them, you must be able to truly feel for, and along with them. In feeling so much, your own inner tranquillity must be disturbed.

This is as it should be. With and through others you once again begin the journey of enlightenment, the path of the fool opens before you once more, ripples of uncertainty and unease disturb that inner calm, only this time, love leads you. With your wish, and willingness to share motivating you… wisdom wishes to learn.

God has sent many messengers and teachers to uplift humanity, to raise us to a higher awareness. If God wishes to share himself with us, why should we aspire to such selfishness and only wish to share ourselves with him and not each other? His lesson is simple,… God is love. Love is not selfish and not self. Love has nothing to do with calmness, peace and tranquillity. It has got everything to do with passion, exuberance, joy and excitement. Reaching within is not loves aim! It is reaching without that is it's true purpose. Love does not live alone and isolated, it enfolds, embraces and envelops all of life. Love loves to love and lives not alone If you have found peace and tranquillity you have fled from Gods furnace of love. It is that fire that fuels the soul and drives it forward to a higher level, a purer purpose.

If in your selfish serenity you believe you have taken God's hand, then allow him to guide you back to the turmoil that is true life, and place your hand in anothers to aid and share that life and love. God loves all!... do you think yourself above God? in that you would isolate yourself in solitary sensation! All need a balance, a counterweight. Joy, calmness, peace, goodness etc, and are only understood through their opposites, grief; anger; strife and evil.

Once you are balanced within your self, (not as those profound passages of self- awareness proclaim "In love with yourself"), then, and only then, is it time to realise the teaching in this condition. Without need, desire or reason to grow or progress, there is stagnation. In stagnation all things falter, wither and die... "Rest in Peace".

God, life and love are not, and never will be about stagnation.

Once more you must walk forward from the safety and sanctuary of your solitude, embracing turmoil, tragedy, grief, anger, sadness, doubt and dismay, and once more overcome. This time you do not strive alone but with and for others sake.

There is a God part within you powering and propelling you. This part is true love and pure love. Love is giving with the wish, the want, and the desire, that others have the best, just as God wishes the best for you.
No longer locked within, always giving without.

Our purpose is not to learn to be an individual, but... how to unite, one with the other, in the love of each other and for the love of each other. To know the touch of Gods love and the joy of sharing that love through the eyes, words, feelings, embrace and emotions of another, to join body and soul and to share and spread that truth as wide as possible.
To live in love! Not to "Rest in Peace".

Perhaps...

Perhaps... If I stop seeing evil, baseness and badness in others?
Perhaps... I will stop seeing the same faults in myself?
Perhaps... Once I see beyond the wicked nature of others?
Perhaps... I will see beyond my own wicked nature?
Perhaps... If I can understand what are the causes of wickedness in others?
Perhaps... I will understand what causes it in me?
Perhaps... If I can accept the failings, faults and fears in others?
Perhaps... I can accept them in myself?
Perhaps... If I realise there is greatness and goodness within others?
Perhaps... I will realise there is greatness and goodness in me?
Perhaps... If I always looked for goodness I would be a happier and better person?

Having an illness that is obvious, be it in appearance or behaviour, does not mean the whole body or person is sick. When the problem is identified then treatment can begin. Healing can take place and the body, mind and soul can be brought back into balance, equilibrium and full health.

Perhaps... If we all tried hard enough we could see past this worlds sickness?
Perhaps... We could see the wonder that is the healthy soul of humanity?
Perhaps... One-day people will realise that those who dream of such things see with open eyes. They are not infected with the sickness that blights and blinds
humanity, nor the insanity that creates the diseases of hatred and spite.
Is the doctor who sees beyond the malady mad?
Is he crazy to care about a cure?
Perhaps... In seeing the soul sickness in others we take the first step towards curing ourselves.
Perhaps... One day others will understand...caring is the cure.
Perhaps...??

Understanding – Understanding

The trouble with truly understanding is understanding you cannot understand!
You must first understand that your human condition precludes you from true understanding. Once you understand this, then you truly begin to understand. But… in understanding that, it therefore follows you must be able to move beyond the human condition to another level, a theoretical or spiritually pure level. In understanding purity of thought, you must instantly understand that the human condition is not able to comprehend true spiritual understanding.
We must learn through the human condition of emotional turmoil how to progress spiritually. This turmoil is generated through hope, hate, and happiness, through greed, generosity, gluttony and giving, by taking, talking and tenderness, with anger, apologies, fear and frustration, in jealousy, jeopardy, craving, caring, crying, lying, living and loving.
Trouble is love… real love? Real love is a spiritual condition, an emotional condition that transcends, en-compasses, and expresses itself way beyond the physical and material limitations of the human condition. Real love is loving beyond yourself while remaining aware of your importance in being the individual through which this wonderful love is expressed.

For someone to truly love you in return, you must be worthy of being loved. To be worthy of true love you must have the capacity to receive true love. To have the capacity to receive true love, you must be able to understand it, to understand that to touch true love is to touch the divine and, in touching the divine we touch purity. But…the human condition precludes the capacity to touch purity…or does it?

Can purity only be achieved through the understanding of impurity? Is knowing love a result of understanding hate? Is generosity gained through understanding greed?

Are we giving through getting? Etc, etc…

In other words, is the duality and contradiction of the human condition the manner in and the means through which we enlighten ourselves?

Is the ability to compare the contradictions the path we take to spiritual awareness? Is this the path to true purity of spirit? Is this contemplation of the converse the completion of the circle? And does the completion of the circle contain the capacity to comprehend pure love? Will it therefore gift us the understanding of loving beyond ourselves, and therefore highlight with crystal clear clarity the obvious contradiction between this condition and the present condition of the world, its populace, its creatures and its environment?

The majority of the earth's population has always been struggling, starving, servile, enslaved and asleep. Their situations, the conditions in which they exist leave no time for moralistic meanderings, spiritual speculations or character contemplation. Fear, pain, food shortages, disease and despair do not lend themselves to speculation into matters metaphysical nor deep debates of global proportions

When you are wondering where the next nibble of nourishment may come from, there is no wonder left in the world, the brotherhood of mankind is only for a certain kind of brother and a certain kind of man.
This is an unfortunate truth of the first, second and third world economies. Wisdom wasted and withering as it waits to be implemented wisely, remains... unused, unheeded and unvalued. Western apathy induced by and through mind numbing programming from vastly wealthy sources using media mesmerism, has slain any thinking other than that of self.

Understanding.... true understanding, would instantly rectify this abomination of minority greed, manipulation and injustice. It would bring about the immediate remedy of global unity and equality. All creeds, cultures, races and religions, and each and every individual within them wanting, wishing and working towards fairness in the distribution of all the earth's riches and resources.
Love leading to understanding that when one suffers we all suffer, love learned and leading to equilibrium, to.... Heaven on Earth?
Hate, hates. Hate hates understanding, it hates tenderness, compassion, care, concern, kindness, thoughtfulness and most especially, hate hates LOVE! Hate takes, it cannot and does not... give. Once you can understand hate, only then will you truly begin to understand love.
To truly understand love, is to truly understand.
The trouble with truly understanding is understanding that you cannot under...

Life

MEMENTOS

I have walked on many paths,
I have travelled many mind miles.
That which endures I carry still,
The friendship and the smiles.

GREEN GRASS

I've made it!
I've done it!
Found fortune and fame.
And it's just so ... And it's just like...
Christ! It's all just the same

The Boxer

Took a look about me,
At the audience in the hall.
Tried to turn and run back,
The path had grown too small.
A twisted taped message,
Runs a feed back through my head.
Couldn't find the exit,
Boxer fights instead.
Eager for understanding,
Bursting to know life's truth,
Moonshine lights the bedroom,
In the head of the constant youth.
My teardrop forms a small boy,
Standing in self-conscious pain.
Laughter from the ladies!
Boxer fights again.
Life fought never harder,
Often on the floor,
Scars upon the memory,
From all the rounds before.
Loneliness is a cold sheet,
Dark nights on your own,
Lover left the corner,
Boxer fights alone.
Punch drunk with the beatings,
Weary to the bone,
Washed upon the rocks of time,
Lashed by human foam.
No place left to turn too,
Locks on people's door,
Weeping for the children,
The boxer fights once more.

THE WHISPERER

My name has been said in secret and dread,
I'm from the land of the dying star.
In filth and in mire, I arise with desire,
I lean close but feel from afar.

I teach the eager young, the uncouth tongue,
I'm the mindless, the madness, the might.
I'm the furious fire, your soul's blackened pyre,
I loiter each long, longing night.

I'm your desperate deeds, your self-staining needs,
I maul minds, I murder, I maim.
I twist and I squirm, inside you I worm,
I lay waste to what goodness you claim.

Indulge and you'll see, you reflect me,
I'm the mirror contorting the whole.
I'm your plague and your blight, the shutter of light,
I snigger as I suck off your soul.

You cannot hope! You cannot cope!
I'm the desperate dealer of dreams.
I'm cunning and sly; it's in your wanting I lie,
I'm the sweetest spewer of schemes.

I'll spin and I'll turn, make your mind burn,
I'll feed from your foulest of foods.
I'll sup from your sores, ooze through your pores,
I'm the bitter that festers your moods.

I'll make life seem so bad, make what's good appear
sad,
I'm the shadow who shortens the wait.
I will feed from your need; I'll fulfil your greed,
I'm the dangler with the lure and the bait.

Don't claim you don't know! It's through you that I
grow,
You're a member of the sect of the sin.
You joined by your hate, avarice your estate,
You looked out but never within.

I answered your call, to be there when you fall,
Your wanting wished me to be.
I gave your disguise a truth full of lies,
I wove the web through which you could see.

Eyes that see true are no good to you,
Tears tend to let the truth leak.
Now you owe me so much, you're well out of touch,
And the dumb have no voice to speak.

You asked and I gave; now I'll dance on your grave,
I'll be patient as your candlelight flares.
You gluttonous glob, self-serving slob,
Do you really think anyone cares?

I wait and I linger, then … pride points a finger,
How early a fool marks their fate.
That superior sneer drew me so near,
You're an addict who just couldn't wait.

I've plenty of space for all of your race,
I harvest in ripe fields of woe.
I'm so glad you were bad, what a good time you had,
How I savour the sourness you sow.

Remember the child? Imagination runs wild.
The Boogie Man under the bed.
Those nursery rhymes, scariest times,
There was truth in every verse said.

You searched and sought, now in my snare you are
caught,
You dealt in the darkest of deeds.
You never realised nor opened your eyes,
Darkness births the growth of all seeds.

They strain for the light; no one tells them it's right,
Yet it yields the power to grow.
In their secular shell, they hear life's wishing spell,
In a seed's song a forest may flow.

But I'm the fancy the flirt; keep you covered in dirt,
I'm the harvest you never will reap,
The wizened willow of hate, the stunted growth state,
The promise you never can keep.

I'll slake your thirst, always putting you first,
You'll not suffer from want or despair.
You'll believe that you must, crave; envy and lust,
I'll make sure you get more than your share.

I'll be the glittering prize, the green gleam in your eyes,
I'm the rainbow with unending fool's gold.
I'm the crest of your kind, no heart and no mind,
The furnace eternally cold.

There are others I see who are no use to me,
They follow the dim distant star.
In their own pain they see, the wings which set free,
Their backs bear another man's scar.

In their eyes lie a tear, yet no doubt and no fear,
What comes they bear as their lot.
They struggle and strive, keep faith alive,
Thankful for the pittance they've got.

I cannot deceive those who believe,
To help others is helping themselves.
If stranger or friend, on you can depend,
Therein lies life's greatest wealth.

So I'll cling to the bland, from them I'll demand,
They'll rush to my beck and my call.
You cannot ignore, for I see in your core,
The molehill from which you must fall.

Be at your ease, I give only to please,
Delight in the values of vain.
Enjoy while you can, this brief lifetime span,
Delight in not feeling the pain.

I will wait in the wings as your short life-song sings,
I'll not hasten that final note.
But my smile will grow, for in that moment you'll
know,
It's over your soul I will gloat.

In that instant you'll see, not only me
But the one that could have been you.
How I savour this part, the last beat of the heart,
As you finally see what is true.

It's crippling to find you've lived your life blind,
To be fooled was ever your fate.
You thought yourself wise, now your lost spirit cries,
As it hangs on your life cross of hate.

Now my face stands revealed, my secret unsealed,
How I love that last gasp of surprise.
You believed till the end in your dark angel friend,
But it's you, watching you, with your eyes.

My name has been said in secret and dread,
By each woman and man it is known.
You may breathe yet not live, if my name you can't
give,
For my name…? It's always your own.

STUNTED GROWTH

What's the bit?

Why the shit?

Who are you trying to fool?

Your 'I don't care' face,

You've no style or grace,

Still you're acting cool

You've not seen,

Or been,

You're soft,

Acting mean.

A learner who'll never know.

Take a real look at yourself,

You're in a box on a shelf.

You'll age,

But never grow.

DRIFTER'S DREAM

Pack my rags,
Grab my bags,
Leave another place called home.
Look at streetlights,
Dark city nights,
There's beauty in my dome.

Endless tar,
Passing car,
Service café's mugs of tea.
Another place,
Another face,
Drivers talk to me.

What a life, it's nice here by the roadside,
Drifting round, just a strange face by the wayside.

Friends I've met,
Don't forget,
I'm a welcome passing person.
Stop a while,
Gab and smile,
It's getting late, I'd better press on.

People fear,
Whisper in my ear,
Think I'm backing off from life now.
Say "settle down,
Get a job in town,
Find yourself a wife now."

"What a life" it's nice here open and free,
Drifting round, there's such a lot to see.

One day perhaps,
I'll leave the tracks,
And take a woman's hand.
But it's hard to find,
A girl my kind,
Whose eyes have sussed this land.

I love my pals,
I love my gals,
I don't want to give or take.
Some will say,
It's a selfish way,
But it's hearts I hate to break.

What a life, it's nice here high and breezy.
Just drifting round, it's the hard times that make it easy.

TO HELL AND BACK

Touched wood,
It's looking good,
Things are going fine.
At last; I thought;
I've found what I sought.
The sun is gonna shine,
Left the hassle,
Tempting tassel,
Plastic smiling face,
The cruel, cool con man,
So fast he's gone, man,
Taking pleasure in my disgrace.
Clutching cuties,
Rooty toot fruities,
Living their life of lies,
Cackling cronies,
Bullshit balonies,
"I believe you," said my disguise.
Presents from a caller,
No good baller,
But I make them feel the best,
My mouth is honey,
My mouth makes money,
My bed does all the rest.
Reached the top,
Couldn't stop,

Trapped by wasted years,
Found my dreams
Were other men's schemes,
Couldn't face the fears.
A needle of hope,
Walked the tightrope,
Monkey bites my skill,
Empty night pain,
Searching for a vein,
The man smiles... can't get my fill.
Rending, tearing,
Cursing, swearing,
Grovelling in the sewer.
Sweating, shaking,
Sanity breaking,
Dying while I cure.
I fell so low,
Had no place to go,
So I jumped a passing craze,
Got into my head,
Good times are dead,
No longer in a daze.
Grew up smart,
Stone cold heart,
Funeral for my youth,
People sigh,
See pie in the sky,
They're born to lose life's truth.
Day's dawn,
Ego gone,

Humanity is just a faker,
Caught my breath,
The next step's death,
And I'm a virgin doomed to take her.
Betrayed by reason,
A brain called treason,
Logic led the way,
I searched and found,
An empty sound.
Games over, no replay.
No good walking,
No good talking,
Individuals need no one.
Know it all,
Cinderella Ball,
Over before it's begun.
No future plan,
Zombie man,
An old man far too soon.
When all is known,
All is blown,
I'm an instrument out of tune.
The seed is sewn,
The last unknown,
Alone on the verge of time,
Don't need to think,
Gaze into the brink,
Then all the verse will rhyme.
Reality spins,
Dimension thins,
"All you have you give,

You've learnt the lie,
You've learnt to die,
Now learn how to live."
A voice in black,
Brought me back,
The contented contradiction,
I knew it all,
'Cause I knew nothing at all,
For the fact is just fiction,
Brave and coy,
Girl and boy,
The outsider in the centre.
Kind and cruel,
Enlightened fool,
Tranquil mind tormentor.
Chameleon man,
Can't and can,
Mirror of every face,
Good and bad,
Sane and mad,
A winner who lost the race.
Look and see,
Look at me,
See yourself within.
You're on neutral ground,
I'm an echo sound,
An ending called begin.

LEGEND OF THE LOST.

Went up in smoke,

Or a head full of coke,

A mind full of double-dealing.

Went up in flames,

Into empty brained dames,

The act that has no feeling.

Sailed away on a rail,

A yesterday's tale,

Young brains skim off my cream.

Head of hope,

Backed up by dope,

Who wants a second hand dream?

Snort and sneeze,

Smoke and wheeze,

Body at different speeds.

The walking blind,

Don't seem to mind,

A dead man has no needs.

THOUGHTS
OF
LOST LOVE.

My mind slips back softly to last summer.
To a countryside bright with sunshine haze.
To a tree with built in cushioned couches,
Where we sat watching nature as we lazed.
How we laughed, how we talked, it felt good girl.
How tightly we held each other's hand.
Your eyes smiling… sparkling,
Sharing things only we could understand.
Memory slams my head, sends blood rushing,
Like the time when through the woods we raced,
Lungs so filled with laughter,
A lasting kiss in our haste.
Light was the body I cradled,
The last time in tree couch we lay,
I wiped a tear from your eye princess,
For us, no words left to say.
A soft sigh like the wind in river reeds,
Blind blue eyes in your golden head,
You drank too deep of natures dream flower,
Nature, come claim your dead.

CAUGHT IN MY CUPS

How many glasses do I have to drink
before I find the bottom?

MEMOIRS

Dark hour comes with cruel cup.
Night once again tempts me sup.
Loneliness brings me close to you,
Love raises cup to lip.

Sensual Sense

SENSING SEX

To please a woman,
You must listen with your fingertips!

THE 'G' SPOT

Stimulate what's between the ears,
And ecstasy between the legs is easy!

SEXUAL FANTASY

Satisfaction in the groin region
May still leave the cranium craving

SEXUAL SATISFACTION

It's wonderful to see lust in your eyes,
Knowing love will linger later.

SEXUAL SATISFACTION II

Your pleasure pleasures me.

OVER INDULGENCE

Sex is xes backwards,
And excess is always unrewarding.

EROTICA EXPLAINED

I reached through 'tantric sex' the highest pinnacle.
Through abstinence, meditation and force of will,
I learnt to control my body and my mind to such a high
degree
That I could induce the most euphoric, intense, lasting
multiple climaxes ever known.
Of course!
I would swap it all for a real live screw
With a bird in suspender belt and stockings!

SEX WITH THE SEXLESS

You marred your inner secret self,
You spoilt your purest seed.
You really thought you gave so much,
You only fed your need.

Sensed

MUDDLED MOTTO

Ignorance is bliss.
Love of my life, here's a passionless kiss.

HONESTY IN LOVE

I would love to have loved you.

ALMOST.

Missed by a mile my love,
Missed by a smile my love,
So near you went out of focus.

JUST THINKING

Dark night,
Coke can,
Rocking in the wind.
Bent,
Used,
Unwanted.
Red,
Bright red,
Waiting to rust,
I thought of modern man.

FOR CHARITY

Black ink stamped headliner,
Coloured paper poster watcher,
People's protest marching cause,
TV's big show interest story,
Donation collector's bread and butter,
Conscience calming child of need,
So much depends on you,
Keep up the good work!
Keep starving!

CARE IN THE COMMUNITY

I lifted up a cardboard lid, underneath a man lay hid.
He was cold and hungry; I was feeling kind.
I closed the lid and closed my mind.

CRIME AND PUNISHMENT

Don't judge another until you uncover,
The same root in your own ego tree.
And don't get a surprise, when you then realise,
You are the guilty one still running free.

MASOCHIST MOB

Stood in a bar room,

And greased my throat some more,

Young kid with a burst mouth came sprawling 'cross
the floor.

Beer bully-boys vied, to bruise his pretty face,

Women pressed forward, looking ugly in white lace.

. "Please!" said the young kid; "what did I do to you?"

He was answered by feeling his children crushed

By a blow from a steel capped shoe.

A question dashed around my brain,

"Should I leave my sheltered corner and help him in his
pain?

Which would be the harder - his beating or my shame?"

The problem was soon unravelled.

A pointed finger gave me the smear.

"Look...! here is another one in the shadows over
here,"

I felt only pity, for as the man machine drew near,

I saw in each and every eye

The herd look of unknown fear.

Later when all was over,

Lying on the cold floor tiling,

My ears still heard the voice of the mob

"Look he's still smiling,"

"Why is he smiling like that?"

"Hit him hard, knock him flat"

"What is he smiling about?"

"Break his arm, make him shout"

"How can he smile still?"

"Make him stop, KILL! KILL! KILL!"

They beat themselves so hard.

"THUMP!"
The fist of fury raised its voice,
It had no chance; it had no choice.
The candle only glowing dim, in spite - kicked out the
light in him!

SMIRK

Don't look so worldly wise tomorrow.
When you fool yourself,
You fool life.

WHAT?

Don't be arrogant in you ignorance tomorrow,
Be inspired!
Be indolent!
Whatever that is...

WORD BLINDNESS

So hard to write.
So hard to right?

PARABLE FROM A BARMAN

You!

You embarrassed me!

You!

With your filthy, ragged, raincoat,

Your drink sodden mind.

I...

I had to make you leave!

I know it's warm here,

But it's part of my job.

"How did you get so thin?"

Why?

Why did you refuse?

I felt stupid using force.

Using it on you.

You!

Old, Weak,

Weak and wretched,

Didn't you see it's for them?

Comfort, Warmth, Laughter.

For them!

Drinks, soft seats.

For them!

Companionship.

For them!

Not for you,

They pay!

Pay to keep you hidden,

Out of sight,

Away,

Go!

Go back to the night,

Please!

You!

You brought coldness,

Loneliness,

Guilt.

I...

I had to be hard,

You made them Uneasy,

"Oh God!"... You...

You embarrassed me!

COMMUNICATION BREAKDOWN

As I stood there dwelling upon life's lot,

It suddenly occurred "what a great lot I got."

Inflamed with this knowledge of brave new dimensions,

To enlighten fellow man was my sincerest intentions.

So on entering a bar room of good stout mankind,

I endeavoured to bring; sight to the blind,

And on calling to all that they gather round,

Proceeded to give forth oration profound.

"Brothers! Men folk! I've come here with joy.

No. I'm not a pusher, you silly little boy,

I bring you the answer that fits like a glove.

And the answer is this…! your fellow man to love."

Oh! My heart skipped a beat.

I scarce thought I'd die,

When all in the bar room with one voice did cry,

A shout so loud, it near lifted the roof,

As in unison they sang out,

"Piss off you poof!"

PHILOSOPHER

I don't like poseur's poofs or dykes!
I don't like blacks or their likes!
I don't like women with too much lip!
I don't like wide boys who think they're hip!
I don't like high brows or college gits!
I don't like swots; they get on my tits!
I don't like those who use fancy words!
I don't like them or their snotty birds!
I don't like prats that seek insight!
I don't like poets they all talk shite!
I don't like aristo's or that blue blood crew!
I don't like the rich; they piss me off, too!
I don't like mouths with too much to say!
I don't like anyone getting in my way!
I don't like cowards who don't stand and fight!
I will not argue when I think I'm right!
I don't like the people who mock what I say!
I don't like the laughter pointed my way!
I don't like politics, religions or rules!
I don't like art, it's crap made for fools!
I don't like loneliness or thinking too deep!
I don't like the time when I'm nearly asleep!
I'm proud that I'm me; I speak open and plain.
Like so many others, I've no doubts and no brain!

EGOTISM

On the page that is your life,
God suffered writer's block!

IN SYMPATHY

"Hey man! Sorry to hear your mind died yesterday!"

FROST BITE

I cannot write or put to page,
Words, which unlock your self-made cage.
Bars of bitterness, dungeons of doubt.
Fear of feeling locks love out.

"TICK"

Just for an instant I lingered in the ruins of recall,

Memory moved me backwards,

Lost lists,

Lost names,

Lost loves,

Childhood games,

Sunrise, Sunset,

Time immovable.

Reflecting,

Age,

The inner clock clicks,

Churns,

Then moves on.

Moment miser,

Knowing only eternity.

Yet,

It had to tick again.

UGH!

My vocation is violence.
My gift? To grant you pain,
Foot and fist make me exist,
Fury's my domain.

Not for me the tender touch,
Diplomacy or care.
A sudden surge; the punching purge,
Blood spurting through the air.

Come meek, come might, come many.
Brute force blinds and mists my eye.
Savage sense is my defence,
Cruelty my war cry.

I stand while others run.
Suffering fills and fuels my force.
Wounds I bear for your despair.
I never waver in my course.

You'll cower before my onslaught,
Conscience cannot stay my hand.
I'll take your crown; I'll beat you down.
I must be master in my land.

I'm the bravest of the brave boys!
There's no weakness left in me.
I'm strong I'm stout, I bear no doubt.
There's one! Just I, Not we!!!

My rage will reap the rewards.
On threats my throne will thrive.
I never bend nor need a friend.
Alone I will survive.

To maintain my macho mirage,
I can never drop defence.
I can never chance an inner glance,
My failing I may sense

I'll never face the inner terrors,
The cringing coward kept in chain.
I'll not go near, my cage of fear,
I could not bear that pain.

So I'll continue my constant craving.
Feed from fear in another's eyes.
I'll never perceive who I truly deceive,
It's myself that I'll always despise.

THE CLOWN'S CLOAK

"You always seem light hearted,
You always seem to smile.
But life can prove a serious game,
You'll learn that in a while."

"You constantly keep chuckling,
You constantly play the fool.
But life's no laughing matter,
You'll learn that golden rule."

"You look ever on the light side,
You look ever for the fun.
But life's fatal for the frivolous,
You'll learn in the long run."

"You forever look for laughter,
You forever look for jest,
But life's a sobering business,
You'll learn like all the rest."

"You forget it's not some child's game,
You forget we must mature.
But life will educate you,
You'll learn of that I'm sure."

I had listened very quietly,
To his grave and earnest lore.
I tried to keep my face straight,
I couldn't manage any more.

The titter ran from head to toe tip,
"I'm afraid it's you who has been fooled.
To find life's mirth and merriment,
First in pain you must be schooled."

It's not joy that makes the joker,
It's the aching deep inside.
It's this grief that gets us grinning,
Then we give to those outside.

In our laughter lies great loneliness,
Long nights groping in the dark.
In the ashes of our ego,
We found a smiling spark.

Life's hard and harsh and hurtful,
Full of tragedy and tears.
But don't make yourself a monument,
To disappointment, doubt, and fears.

Each has their load to carry,
Each has their cross to bear.
Why are you adding to their burden?
With that woeful face you wear?

Sometimes people need an ear to listen,
Sometimes they need a tender touch.
But the gift of giving a giggle,
Often means as much.

Laughter loosens sorrow's strangle,
It may lighten a sad soul's load.
To join in joy with one another,
May ease a lonely road.

There is a hidden hook in a clown's cloak,
Once worn it's on for life.
'Sardonicus' always smiling,
Can never show his strife.

Pause a moment on the comic,
What price his merry mask?
What lesson in his laughter?
What teardrops in his task?

But seriously, don't start laughing,
Don't mock now; do not scoff.
One day I may get lucky,
And laugh my fool head off!

LIFE CYCLE

Almost the hoops complete now,

This circle cycle of my life.

The cyclones eye is clear to me,

There's calm where once was strife.

So many rings I had to jump through,

Spinning wheel within a wheel.

Those roundabouts of ruin,

Taught me what was real.

Often on those orbits,

I believed the end I'd gain.

Until yet another spiral,

Began to turn again.

Each cycle had conclusion,
On each loop towards a man.
I found truths child before me,
I was back where I Began.

Revolutions revealing revelations,
Hoops of learning for my soul.
Now chain link all together,
To the boy who once was whole.

The error was first to question,
Then to search for a reply.
A Childs loves pure and simple,
All else was but a lie.

Now a man looks from the mirror,
Age and wisdom his disguise.
Inside an infant giggles,
And love lights up his eyes.

THE END OF LIFE ! ! !

LEARNING

DAWN

I began to hope again,

I began to dream.

I began to plan again,

It began to mean.

I started to remember,

I started to forget.

I started to look forward,

To days not come as yet.

CONTRARY

Am I going forward?

Or am I going back?

Did I catch the right train?

While on the wrong track?

Did I find the real truth?

Or find real truth a lie?

Am I learning how to live?

Or learning how to die?

Did I get here too early?

Did I arrive too late?

Is the unknown question the answer...?

To a well planned fate?

Is giving a way of getting?

Or just a way of being nice?

Did I ask you all these questions?

Just to give you my advice?

LOOKING IN THE MIRROR

So you think; I think; I know it all,
I only strive to prove me right.
You must have gained a higher ground,
Which grants a further sight?

And when you stand on this higher ground,
And hear that higher call,
Then surely you must realise
You too are a… 'know it all.'

LOOKING IN THE MIRROR (AGAIN)

Look at Me! I stand straight and true.
You could not conceive what I've been through.
Hold on! You could, you've been there too!
I was thinking of me, while really thinking of you.

YOUR MIRROR

It's only you, you doubt,
When you wonder what I'm all about

WHAT'S WITH THIS MIRROR?

How extraordinary to realise you're so ordinary

MENTAL BLOCK

The mirror replied,

I'm not sure who lied?

My reflection or my brain?

How can it be?

Why can't I see?

MYSELF???

WISE WORDS FROM THE WATCHER

I see you, I really do.

I see in me what you think is you.

REFLECTING

The hot sun bronzed the waters still,
As I lazed by my secret lake.
How deep did its reflective skin?
This worldly image take?

Calm, serene, it posed itself.
No ripple marred its face.
Yet underneath life raged within,
A hidden inner pace.

Sudden surge sent stone a-spin,
To splash and scar its mask.
A sudden sadness for the act,
Drew my mind to task.

Did my secret pool mirror to close?
My life in this world outside?
A false facade, a thin veneer,
A visage 'neath which I hide.

Within this form a billion lives
Survive on the air I breath.
Within this form is the soul of man,
But its depth I can't perceive.

I realised the tutor of truth,
Stood whispering in my ear.
Words unsaid spoke in my head,
"It's themselves that all men fear."

DOUBT

My heart keeps time to the beat,
Throbs in my head,
Throbs in my feet.
The wallflower wanting to dance.

SNOWDROP.

Lady, I loved you as a memory,
From the very start.
I knew we'd plan together,
But I knew that we would part.
For springtime was within you,
As you thought to be my wife.
I would have only killed that blossom,
With the winter in my life.
Yet, even the hardest winter,
Can feel the hint of spring.
It awakens forgotten memories,
And fresh hopes will it bring.
Now, this long lonely winter is passing,
There's a thaw on an ice-cold heart.
And a tear falls from an icicle,
For a lost spring that made it start.

LOSING YOU
I cried,
And the teardrop was a lie.

IT'S

It's only rage that fills this page,
It's frustration that's slamming my head,
It's my human side, my stupid pride,
It's the lonely each night in my bed,
It's knowing too much, when another's eyes touch,
It's the needing forever to give,
It's dancing in mire, knowing greed and desire,
It's loving and loving to live,
It's the needing to feel, trying to heal,
It's wanting, and waiting and need,
It's knowing you're growing and hunger you're sowing,
It's a famine you never can feed.

STRIVING FOR STATUS

When the ego eats, your soul grows thin.
A golden bucket is still a rubbish bin!

THE FARCE OF FAECES

When I was a child, I was ever so shy,
But as I got older with my masks I got by.
With the aid of this make-up, I always would fit,
Even dealers in shit still want the best bit.
Then one day a man said,
"You're top of the pile."
The fact sudden dawned and gave me to smile,
I wallowed and waded, seen the envious eyes.
The crowned King of Crap was a sought after prize.
How others envied, and vied for my crown,
The thing was 'being',
And the 'being' was brown.
For years I protected my hoard of manure,
Until one day I realised,
I wasn't so sure…?
Why did I strive to stay at the top?
Why was I happy with crap for a crop?
So I gave away my mountain of stools,
Was I the fool, on the path of the fools?
Yet I walked away saving not even a fart,
From that day forth a new life I did start.
The way has been hard, yet I'm happy inside.
I still stink of the sewer but I don't wear it with pride.
It's a badge of beginning the blast from the bowel
To know what smells sweet is to know you've smelled
foul.

STILL SEARCHING

I know.

I know the answer.

I saw the light; I know the way.

I have wisdom; I have insight,

I know just what to say.

I could answer all the questions,

I could banish all the doubt,

I could enlighten every person,

If I knew what I was on about.

LEARNT

I stand still,
Eyelids fill,
Gazing in my grave,
Trying to be brave.

All alone,
Engaged tone,
My number is never free,
You cannot contact me,
I'm alone as alone can be.

I have laughed,
I have cried,
I have stood outside,
Swallowing my pride.

Loved a lot,
Cool and hot,
All ways and all kinds,
Even loved some minds,
Surprising what one finds

Pulled my head apart,
Back to my start,
Searching for lost dreams.
Memory madly screams.

Grinding gears.
Subconscious fears,
Brain out of control,
Sanity drills a hole,
Burrowing like a mole.

Round the bend,
Will it ever end?
Mentality runs amok,
My eyes now have a lock.

Oblivion skull,
Dreary and dull,
Life now lies in shreds,
I've a multitude of heads,
Such loosely woven threads.

A God cried, a man died,
I think it was one of me,
I couldn't really see
There was thirty-three to tea,
And all of them were me.

Twilight shapes,
Eternity waits,
Madness moves my mind,
Normality I cannot find.

Feel your heart; fall apart,
Squeeze it gently,
Catch the tear,
See the inside fear.

I spy,
With a rummy eye,
The child behind the veils,
Tomorrow's unfilled sails,
Yesterday's certain trails.

I have lived,
I have loved,
I have learnt to stand aside,
Swallowing my pride,
With the multitude inside,
Knowing I'm not really me,
Has taught me how to be,
Free.

MAYBE MATURE

The man said he'd grown up,
And so it would seem,
But I think he just gave up,
On his great childhood dream

ENDLESS THIRST

I once thought that I knew it all,
Now… I know I did,
But I unlocked Pandora's box,
Now… I cannot close the lid.

ENLIGHTENMENT

I've seen behind the last hidden door,
Want to know what's there?
A room with doors galore!

A.B.C.

Persistent voices entwine my head,
Hours ago I should have curled in bed.
But constant questions fill my ear,
Stay my eyes open; keep me here.
Years have taught me the right things to say,
But another man's thoughts won't show you your way.
A million truths can't teach you what's right,
Yet one little lie may blot out the light.
What are the sounds that lie in the heart?
If we could utter its voice we would not stand apart.
Peel back all of your masks; see the true face.
Isn't that strange! You're the whole human race!
The river of life has a true course to follow,
Be certain of love, of joy and great sorrow.
Increasing your wisdom still leaves you yearning,
As each answer opens more paths of learning.
It's a hope that keeps rising and could make nations follow,
And it's knowing the focus would be human and hollow.
It's the devil that rides you and keeps you in doubt,
In the great maze of life, truth's the way out.
Give all that you can, then, give even more.
You'll never run out, love's a limitless store.
Take all of the hurt, but learn from the pain.
And if you learn well, it's yourself you may gain.

DREAMER

Once upon a time, a handsome Prince,

On a steed of snorting steel,

Whisked the maiden away to Fairy Land,

Where all the dreams were real.

"From this day forth", the Prince did say,

"Happiness is all you know,

All dreams you have will come to pass,

And no older shall you grow."

Years sped by in contented bliss no worries on her mind.

The maiden lived her dreams each day,

With her Prince, who was loving and kind.

Now it came to pass while wandering,

around that fairyland flat,

She came upon a looking glass,

before which the Prince oft sat.

"This is the window on the world outside…!

All can be seen," said a voice.

Now, for the first time in many a year,

For herself she had a choice.

Never again the maid realised,

would her dream world be content,

Until she had gazed in this mirror of mist,

In which visions came and went.

Time passed by,

Her mind was confused,

But already the maid did know,

That come dark of night, under guiding moonlight,

To that misty mirror she'd go.

And so it happened, the maid peered in,

To see that life she'd fled.

Down and down her mind was drawn,

To a past she thought was dead.

'Neath blue black sky, gem studded with stars,

And the wind upon her gown,

Strolled the maid of content, from ever after world,

Upon her brow a frown?

To a small town came she, while all were asleep,

'Twas lamp light lit her way,

There she heard a song on the breeze,

From a voice both sweet and gay.

Sudden soft and sad turned the song,

Bitter… yet sweet were the tears in her eyes,

For the words of the song were older than time,

From a young man very world wise.

"Come!" said the maid, "I'll take you away,

Sadness no more will you feel,

For I live in a land where no worries are known,

And all the dreams are real."

The young man smiled and shook his head,

"Thank you miss, but no;

It's by knowing sadness that I know gladness,

I have no need to go."

"By facing fears, by shedding tears,
True happiness comes to me.
To know what's right... is to know what's wrong,
In looking you learn to see.
If in dreamland you stay with no worries or cares,
It's life you'll cease to feel.
It's only by keeping in touch with life,
That you know the dream to be real."

"Fairyland's true; I know this for a fact,
Please believe the things I've said."
The maid knew it true, for deep in his eyes,
She saw fairyland... in his head.
Suddenly...! The Prince appeared
And filled them both with fear.
No longer soft spoken and handsome was he.
As he spoke with a vicious sneer.

"So you dared to look in the mirror of truth,

And leave my realms of dreams,

Now pain shall you know, and worry and woe,

For nothing is as it seems."

A red ball of light smashed the silken night,

Noise crashed in the maiden's ear,

Her world fell apart; fear clutched her heart

As she clung to a life now dear.

Long held she on, then…on hearing a song,

She awoke at home in her bed.

A dream…? Perhaps!

But she's glad to be back,

to a life she thought was dead.

Now the maid's often seen,

Hand in hand with a young man,

who sings both sad and gay.

To people it seems, they are living in dreams,

Can you live life any other way?

I KNOW WHO I'M NOT

How much can I hold; can my mind enfold?
Can this universe fit in my head?
I search and I seek, neath' all stones I peek
And file it each night while in bed.

The dawn of time, emerging from slime,
Eternity beckons from space.
Forward or back, they're both the same track,
It's now that I somehow must face.

A twitch of light in never ending night,
Is this all that being can mean?
A second on, then forever gone,
I may as well never have been.
Why am I me? What do I see?
Why ponder on what cannot be known?
Cursed by, WHY?
Unable to lie,
With each answer the question has grown.

I know I can't know, yet my search doesn't slow,
There's some reason I cannot quite see.
Reality recoils, my sanity boils.
I don't know who's the me within me!

Who masters my mind, makes me this kind?
Who drives me to drink or desire?
Who puts these words in my head, dreams in my bed?
Is my brain just a taxi for hire?

Why can't I see the man that is me?
Who determines what mood I will take?
Happy or sad, keep calm or go mad,
It's a choice, which the other will make.

Words tumble out, through my mouth they spout,
But they're formed from somewhere within.
I try to relay the feelings I say,
My voice covers the soul sense with sound.

Vocals can't frame; it isn't the same,
Emotions do not have a voice.
Eyes say much more, it's from inside they pour,
Speech is the liar's choice.

I do not know … from what source does this flow?
Who powers this pen and this ink?
I wait and see, as this hand is set free,
I don't command what this mind may think.

Who's in control, subconscious or soul?
Who's selecting the next thought to come?
That other inside, he will decide,
I just march to the beat of his drum.

Is it neutron and nerve this Master I serve?
Who put the thought that I'm thinking in me?
A computer of a kind, a meat machine mind?
I function... but who's pressing the key?

I don't tell my heart, to stop or to start,
I don't tell my lungs to take air.
My body makes its own way through
each night and day,
And within is its own self-repair.

I don't realise all that enters my eyes,
The calculations that are constantly made.
The movements I make, judgements I take,
I'm just the stage on which the drama is played.

Is it Devil or God who gives me the prod?
Who evokes the joy or the tear?
Why can't I find, the real mastermind?
Who's the driver who puts me in gear?

There is one thing I know as I constantly grow,
I'm not the author, but I can choose my part.
It's all up to me, just what I will be,
A seedling is only the start.

I hope that I'm right as I reach for the light,
There is much, which could keep me in shade.
But at the end of the day, I carve my own way,
I'm not the swordsman, But... I am the blade.

In each human soul is the broken and whole,
The least and the greatest of man.
The designer inside will not let me hide,
I must strive to be the best that I can.

YOUR KNIFE HURTS

Why blame me for the things you don't do?
Why punish me for the guilt within you?

SHARING
(more muddled motto's)

It's not better to give than receive…!
It's better to share!
Sharing another's pleasure when you give…
is a reward in itself.
Allow another to share that same pleasure
when you receive.
It's better to share… than give or receive.

PROPAGANDA

It's the ability to accept comfortable,
That allows the lice of lies to breed in your head.

WISDOM

I'm going to divulge the secret of the wise,

There's no cryptic message, it's the truth, no disguise,

If you wish for power or you wish to do good,

You must influence people;

you must put them in 'mood'.

Your masks may be many; the herd's easy to lead,

Show them your cross; show how hard you can bleed.

Give them desire, a concern or a cause,

Give them a hope and dreams without pause.

Billions are waiting; eating lies every day,

They vote with their crotch, it's freedom they say.

We've advanced, we've grown rich,

we decide what will be,

Entrapped by yearning, we still claim to be free.

Thousands of years of wanting and need,
And all that we've learnt is the power of self-greed.
So I'll shatter your bonds, I'll sever your ties
I will once again utter the words of the wise.

You'll not find them in bibles or temples or creeds,
You'll not find them in others or actions or deeds,
You'll not find them in glory, in pride or in pain,
You'll not find them at all if you are looking for gain.

Look deep in your eye to the soul seed of truth,
There lies the master still teaching the youth.
The wisdom of ages, the secret profound,
It lies not without, it's within it is found.

You were born with life's truth
then were taught all the lies,
The path to yourself is the way of the wise.

PERSONAL RESPONSIBILITY

They say I have the option,
They say I have a choice,
But who are they?
How can they say, I hear an inner voice?

I don't choose what I will care for,
Something moves within my heart,
I don't choose with whom I'll linger,
Something tells me I must part.

I don't choose how you will hear me,
Something moves within your mind,
I don't choose how you will see me,
Something tells you what to find.

I don't choose who I come close to,
Something links... we share a smile,
I don't choose who will dislike me,
Something misses by a mile.

I don't choose to be a lover,
Something trembles deep within,
I don't choose to be alone at night,
Something painful starts to spin.

I don't choose to be a writer,
Something moves my hand to pen,
I don't choose to share my inner self,
Something speaks... I write again.

I don't choose the way my mind works,
Something craves then seeks for more,
I don't choose the path I've taken,
Something opened up the door.

I don't choose this constant searching,
Something causes me to seek,
I don't choose this constant question,
Something drives me when I'm weak.

I don't choose to feel my brother,
Something lies heavy on my soul,
I don't choose to feel my sister,
Something aches; I pay the toll.

I don't choose yet I'm the master,
Of my fortune and my fate,
I don't choose yet something tells me,
I chose love instead of hate.

CANCEROUS
CONVERSATIONS

Do you know how much your words weigh?
Do you know they can hurt or heal?
Do you know that each carries much magic?
They cast a spell, which others will feel.

Be always aware every time you are speaking,
Of the meaning in each word that you say.
Put your honesty into every sentence,
And keep self-opinions at bay.

Many mouths mutter mischief and malice,
Gossips filled with fear and despite,
So sure their own viewpoint is valid,
So certain their reasoning's right.

Conceit it carries a cancer,
It rots, it ruins, It kills.
And if you deal in deadly diseases,
You can be sure to catch some of its ills.

Wicked whispers wound not only the victim,

They fester in the soul of their source.

Poison pours out in petulant prattle,

Vitriol burns all in its course.

First be sure before voicing your belief,

Or passing judgement on anyone's life.

That you understand the load that they carry,

And will not add to their burden and strife.

How many adults still carry from childhood?

A cruel taunt that cut them so deep.

Be very watchful of words to the young child,

Don't cause a wound that forever they'll keep.

Let laughter and love be your language,

Bring compassion and care when you call.

Remember...! When you have nothing good to say,

It's much better to say nothing at all.

WET WISDOM

I weep.

Raindrops of reality.

Life's painful punctuation points.

Soul seepage,

Little lakes of learning?

Dew drops of a new dawn,

Moisture of meaning,

Flowing feelings,

Liquid love,

Rivers of release,

Pearls of pity,

Damp doubts,

Drops of dismay,

Tears that teach?

Wet wisdom.

FLEA BITES

Where now those fields of flowers?
Where now the childhood wood?
A car park and a fast food store,
Where once the oak tree stood.

Where now the teeming tadpole pond?
Where now the field mouse nest?
A business park; a concrete grave!
They're gone like all the rest.

Where now the days of summer long?
Where now the warm night sky?
Cars now choke the air I breathe,
And bright lights blind my eye.

Where now from here can we go?
Where now do we advance?
So much we lost and thought we'd gained,
We continue in this trance.

Where now those fields of poppies?
Where now those that gave their all?
So many fell for sacred soil,
On which now building bricks stand tall.

Where now is our future?
Where now does man turn to?
We've nearly used up nature's store,
What then will mankind do???

Where now will man's greed lead to?
Where now can we all flee?
Ancient earth will cleanse itself!
From parasites she'll be free!

MY FRIEND

How well you wear your wisdom guise,
A searching mind behind laughing eyes;
Cheerful face and carefree stance;
Sees so much with that casual glance.

When first did "why" arise in youth?
Unsteady steps on the path towards truth.
What unspoken voice made you first realise?
Wise men listen with open mind; open eyes.

When first did you learn to touch your tears?
When first did you learn they hold every mans fears?
When first did your hurt, your load, your bane?
Awaken awareness to all others pain?

How many stumbles; failures, and falls?
Wanting to stop…inner voice…it still calls!
How many lonely nights with so many around?
How many talking without making a sound?

Learning of yourself, of others, of life.
Into yourself, you plunge the sharp knowledge knife.
Those scars they don't show; features remain fair.
Those that can see; see the scars in your stare.

But the knife that digs deep also cleans as it cuts,
Memory remains marked,
but the wound heals as it shuts.
How often you picked at each scar on each sore,
Your own pain was your teacher;
you wished to know more.

Lessons you learnt well and carried thereafter.
Found the fool in the insight, in misery your laughter.
For the two are entwined; the bitter and sweet;
It's getting your balance; that's the difficult feat.

So ...you have done well, O Masterful one!
The tears they still roll, but mostly in fun.
As you already know, you will learn till the end.
It's a privilege to know you; and call you ...
"my friend".

THE ANVIL
Friendships are forged in forever

FAREWELL
No regrets
No tears
Just grateful
For a gift that will never end
Always welcomed
Always with me
Always missed
Always my friend

LEARNING TO LIVE?
OR
LIVING TO LEARN?

LOVE AND LIGHT

DUEL SCARS

Those that care are often wounded,
They bear wounds that never heal.
But they bear those wounds with wisdom,
Those that don't will never feel.

SAPLING

Don't treat my words as rare fruit,
Borne on a sacred tree.
It's my roots in the soul soil of your earth,
That births the flower in me.

LOVE GROWTH

There's a love beyond,
So far beyond,
There's a love I sense,
Yet can't make the bond.

There's a love within,
Every step I take,
There's a love so fine,
Beyond heartbreak.

There's a love I know
I will never touch,
There's a love out-with,
I can't hold that much.

There's a love so cold,
It burns my soul.
I'm part of a jigsaw,
That makes love whole.

There's a love that seeks,
What can't be found.
There's a love that screams!
An empty sound.

There's a love inside,
Which calls once again.
There's a love that smiles,
As I writhe in pain.

There's a love that knows,
Far beyond my night.
There's a love that grows,
With each self-insight.

There's a love for me,
Which is mine alone.
There's a love so vast,
Not yet fully grown.

THE LIE OF LOVE

I can give you all a man can give,
But I cannot give you my life to live

THE LIE OF LOVE II

You said, " you love me, you need me, you'll die".
You want so much I must say goodbye.
You said you loved me, you needed me, you'd die.
Now twenty years later, you too see the lie.

AWAKENINGS

Have you dreamed you'd find a lover?
Hoped and wished to find a friend?
Prayed someday someone would come?
On whose heart you could depend?

Have you longed for words and laughter?
To tell secrets two could share?
Have you wanted to talk about your life?
With someone who would really care?

Have you needed arms to hold you?
Whispers spoken softly in your ear?
Have you needed someone to comfort you?
And help you through your fear?

Have you learnt to bear the lonely?
Have you suffered with the pain?
Have you hurt so bad in the silent night?
Time and time again?

Have you managed to build the barricade?
Have you hidden yourself inside?
Have you stopped your life light burning?
Turning isolation into pride?

Have you lost the gift of giving?
Have you forgotten how to feel?
Have you, through desperation?
Closed your heart with ice cold steel?

Wisdoms wounds are ever open.
They bleed through tear filled eyes.
Yet... not all tears are formed by sadness.
Awake! Let laughter be your prize.

Bear all life has to offer.
See the bad; but see what's good.
Welcome life's painful teacher.
And see the joy beneath his hood.

An open heart is honest.
Sees clearly far and true.
Sees deceit within the strongest.
Be a fool; but don't fool you.

Love stands here right before you!
A friend; a mate; a man!
Step free beyond your self made wall,
Choose life! Live all you can!

FOUND

I've spent my lifetime searching,
Always asking why?
The moment I first saw you,
God gave me his reply.

A FROSTY MORNING

God…! It was cold this morning,
I stood outside; near naked, to watch you leave.
Ready to dance stupidly for your delight
And receive my reward...?
Your warming smile!
You drove away without looking?
God it was cold this morning!

THE MISSING LINK

Loves comes without a warning,
It's there, it fills your frame.
Everything is as it always was,
Yet nothing seems the same.

What's this weight within my belly?
What's this joy, this fear, this pain?
What's this tightness in my chest now?
What's this new piece in my brain?

Why do I always think in 'we' now?
Why do I always think of two?
Why do I always think of her wants?
Why do I always want to do?

How did I live before this?
How did I get through any day?
How did I think I was alive then?
How did I find my way?

There's a missing part I found now,
Of its absence I was unaware.
Love links two lives together,
One life we both now share.

APART

How long is a night without you?
How long is an hour, a day?
How long is the motionless moment?
Tomorrows a lifetime away.

APART ONCE MORE

Time tortures me.
Your leaving still scourging my senses.
The agony of being apart too fresh.
My soul screams.
A child stamps his foot in frustration.
A wise man lost in longing.
Bearing the unbearable.
Staring at the solitary.
Your echoes ripple in my rooms.
Lingering love.
The ache in alone.
So many slow sliding seconds between here;
And the magic of meeting once more.
You're breath, your smile, your eyes, your touch.
YOU!!! You fill the empty in me.
Katrina... I miss you.

APART AGAIN
It's the bliss I miss!

ANOTHER PARTING

Again I leave,
I make my way,
Return and leave you here.
Again I'll miss,
Your lips to kiss;
To hold your body near.

Once more we part,
I leave my heart,
My eyes on other things.
Once more I'll sigh,
Regret goodbye,
On memories my mind clings

Laughter long,
A dreadful song!
A tender loving touch.
Silken thighs,
Shining eyes.
Moments mean so much.

Tomorrow I face,
This human race,
I'll smile, I'll talk, I'll strive.
Drink and eat,
But until again we meet;
I am only half alive.

YOU

You...!!!

You are a lake for my thirsty eyes

ODE TO KATRINA

Of all the women I ever met,
You are the one I could never forget.
Of all the women I've ever met,
You are the one I will never forget.
Of all the women I ever met,
You are the one!!!

BREATHLESS

The first time that I saw you,
There was so much I wished to say.
Words withered on my mouth and lips,
You simply took my breath away.

SOME THINGS

Some things make life much better,
Some things make life worthwhile.
Some things make timeless treasures,
You!
Your warmth!
Your smile!

JOINED

My lovely lady lay with me,
Her body joined with mine.
Together in the sea of love,
We touch what is divine.

My skin still carries scents of her,
My pores have soaked them in.
Part of me now lies with her,
My soul mate, my soul twin.

REALLY MAKING LOVE

To fall asleep between your thighs,
And awake next morning behind your eyes.
To arise with regret and leave loves bed,
But the best of me remains in your head.

To work and wait the hours with regret.
To look forward to what's not come as yet.
To know should time shred this dream apart,
Love's child once created remains in the heart

KNOWN.

Know that when you read this,
Know I think on you.
Know everything I feel is real,
Know all I've said is true.

Know I stand beside you.
Know you never stand-alone.
Know loves root is the strongest.
Know in love all things are grown.

TIMELESSLY AND TRUE

Yesterday, today, tomorrow, and forever.
I love you, and will always love you.
Past, present, and future.
You were, are, and always will be... my love.
Before life, during life, and in afterlife.
I have, do, and will always, love you.
Timelessly and true.

BABY

The miracle of birth has come your way,
This breath of life is here to stay,
A gift so precious, a gift so sweet,
This gift of love makes joy complete.

LOVE LESSON

To truly know love,
You must move from the deceit of the self,
To knowledge of the self.
From knowledge of the self,
To the truth of the self.
In the truth of the self,
Is the dislike of the self.
In the dislike of the self,
Is the honesty of the self.
In the honesty of the self,
Is the love of the self.
In the love of the self,
Is the capacity to love out-with the self.
To love out-with the self…
Is to finally know love.

LOVE LESSON 11

To love someone is easy!
You open a door within your heart,
It has always been within you,
Never ending, no need to start.
It came with you from the soul sea,
It is what and where you will return.
It is all the point in living,
It is all you have to learn.

LOVE LESSON 111

We know nothing,
Until we know love.
I never knew love,
Until I knew you.

THE HERMIT

When I was eighteen I wished to know God, so, I took to a cave and became a hermit.

I lived this way for thirty-eight years thanks to the kindness and generosity of the local populace who respected and revered the holy man in their midst and would each day fill the basket lowered from my isolated cave forty-five feet above; with water; food and the necessities of life.

Each day I spent in contemplation and meditation of the soul, the id, the ego, and awaited patiently God's revelation. Until one great day in my fifty-sixth year, finally I heard and was in the presence of the One God. "Master!" I cried, "I have lived a life of abstinence, loneliness, devotion, deprivation and hardship. I have given my all for this one moment of enlightenment in your divine presence!"

"Contemptuous fool!" came the booming reply. "For all those years I have heard your bleating. In your pride and self-deceit you put yourself above other men. From the sweat of their brows, the modesty of their minds and shame of their sins, you have fed, watered and wasted your life! Ever their eyes would look up towards you in their daily drudge and they would feel lesser in their lust, longing, living and minding the mundane. Ever they spoke with awe of the young man who came so long ago, turning his back on the trivial in life, to come face to face with God.

Each night the prayers that would have been useful elsewhere were directed to you in your saintly solitude, to your abstinence; loneliness; devotion and hardship. You became the rod for every back, each stumble, and each harsh word. All enjoyment or festivity in the area carried you as its load! How could one better themselves? Deal with desire? Enjoy themselves? Aspire to good deeds? While above them existed the one who went without! Without WHAT? The temptation of the bottle! The fantasy made flesh! The working, waiting, wishing and wanting! The misery and misfortune! Heartache and hunger! Feelings and fear! The constant feeding mentally and physically, of family and friends. No!!! Here is your long sought revelation.

Too many nights have I heard your prideful, pious pleas while your stomach was full and your thirst was whetted. Too many nights I have dreaded the drone of what you had done without, never once did I hear what you had done!

So... tonight I reveal myself to you... in disdain... disdain of your deceit and your years of taking. No thought to them as you fed on the fare in the basket, the bread and the brew, the pleas for a prayer, their wishes of well".Too many nights you grated about what you had given up, but never once did I hear what you had given! Too many nights I heard you devote your life to me, of what use is a life that has never been lived? So... tonight I reveal myself to you... in disdain...

disdain of your deceit and your years of taking. No thought to them as you fed on the fare in the basket, the bread and the brew, the pleas for a prayer, their wishes of well".

"You took, and took, and took, every day.

Never once did you think what you could do to repay.

Always concerned with your inner most fear,

'What will I do if God doesn't come near?'

So after all this time I have come to reveal,

You never gave once, so you never did feel.

A life committed to what cannot be known

Each day in that valley they gave what they could.

They gave of their best, their prayers and their food.

No matter their problem, their blight or their woe,

Conscious would call and to your basket they'd go.

Aloof in your eyrie you would haul on the rope,

Your piety shamed them!

They're shame helped you cope.

And so great deceiver at the end of your line,

I reveal the great secret! The will that's divine.

Long have you searched from the roots of your youth,

But the lie that's your life is now enlightened with truth.

In these few years I grant you decide on your fate,

Choose your path wisely before it's too late!"

The village still wonders what made

the hermit come down.

Married and drank in the 'Rose and the Crown'.

Fathered three children, toiled hard every day.

And always had time for laughter and play.

What insight? Revelation? Led him always to smile?

Why a tear in his eye when alone for a while?

No one knew, but all were glad he'd come down.

All enjoyed their new friend in town.

And all were sad at his final demise.

All in that church had tears in their eyes.

"So…! The fool made use of the time that he had.

Living a life both good and bad.

He gave his love to his family, strangers and friends.

And love once started has no limits or ends.

It's easy to duck, to run and to hide,

Hardest of all is to face the you that's inside.

Know that in God's eyes, you're

the miracle made whole,

If you would face God...

Turn your face to your soul !"

A STEP TO THE SOUL

See true

See you

Catch you then free you

Be true

Be you

Find you then free you

Feel true

Feel you

Feel all then free you

Lose true

Lose you

Alone at last

You may find you

HURT OF THE HEALER

My dreams have flown to regions unknown,
It's now in chaos my mind seeks content.
My hand held the knife, which slaughtered my life,
Yet there's peace in this constant torment.
The cross, which I bear, is the mask that you wear,
I'm the wound in which you can heal.
If you rummage around in my mind can be found,
An answer to the pain, which you feel.
I'II touch you inside, wont let you hide,
I'II open doorways that lead you to you.
My knowledge is vast, but changing so fast,
In my darkness your light can shine true.
Please carry your load, before I explode,
Please look, then… look once again.
You ask much of me; look and you'll see,
I'm your answer that cannot explain.
I can ease your plight; give you insight,
I can heal you, and open your eyes.
But don't look in me! there's a dark you can't see,
There's a love, that loves to despise.
No wonder I scream; for that lost child's dream,
No wonder I cannot make sense.
No wonder my pain, seems selfish and vain,
Another's need is always immense!

FOOLISH FEARS

Lots of people think I'm a nutter!

I'm completely off my head.

"You know he speaks to spirits,

Converses with the dead"!

They think I'm off my rocker,

Totally bonkers, Raving mad.

"He used to be so sensible,

It really is quite sad".

If I speak of hands of healing,

Spirit guides or my belief.

They nod their heads politely,

Then leave quickly with relief.

I often feel the pointed finger,

Overhear the muffled laugh.

"People are dying to meet you"

"If it's spirits make mine a half".

But often the jesters the first one,

As long as no other is there to see,

Who anxiously asks the question?

"Em - - - Have you got anything for me"?

So walk this path with confidence.

Your way is ever in the light.

But should they take the mocking too far,

Just say" I see spirit with you, - - -

TONIGHT!!!

ETERNAL FLAME

Often I feel you beside me,
I feel you near while on my own,
Often when I miss you most,
The air whispers, "you're not alone!"

Often when in memory I wander,
The house slowly sighs your name.
Often in those busiest moments,
My hearts time you still claim.

Often loss and longing linger,
Then I reach to hold your hand.
Often then, pain punches hardest,
As I remember... then understand.

Often as the bedroom beckons,
I see your pillow lying bare.
Often I know to my dream you come,
Once again we give and share.

Often now I catch myself musing,
Wondering... asking why?
Often the truth then tells me,
Real love lives, it cannot die!

IN SPIRIT

Memory moves my moments,
So much of you surrounds me still,;
Apart, - but never parted,
I love you and always will.

TROUBLE WITH TENDERNESS

Tenderness tears my throat sometimes,
Cloaks and chokes my voice.
An open heart, an open mind,
Allows no other choice.
To feel and love another,
Binds soul and sense and thought.
Pure pain of perception;
When in another's hurt your caught.
Joy also is a jailor,
Who turns the hearts cell key.
Delight in someone's happiness,
Tender tears set free.
Joy and pain are unified.
Each has their role to play,
To know true love is priceless.
Tenderness! ... It's the price you pay.

CONFUSION

The Jews claim they are chosen,
Mormons do as well,
If I don't convert to Catholic,
I'll surely go to hell.

Buddhist, Hindus, Ba'hais too,
Each hold the truth they say.
Confucius calls many converts,
Confusion bars my way.

Does Islam have the answer?
Zoroaster might be right.
Shinto! Say the Japanese,
Maybe…? It just might.

All claim they've found the pathway,
All others lead to Hades.
There's a deluge worth of dogma,
Through which a seeker wades.

Does one faith hold the secret?

Or is each a jigsaw part?

Is there a greater picture?

Is that picture just the start?

There's a madness driving mankind,

They claim their cause comes from above.

They slaughter non-believers,

Then claim their God is love?

How cruel, how sad, how bitter,

To hate the God of another man.

How strange whilst screaming hatred,

To think you're following God's plan?

We are not moving forward,

We err as much as in the past.

Our eyes feed on the moment,

And the moment cannot last.

Ask me not for answers,
Ask me not who's right.
Ask me not for meaning,
I do not have that sight.

We are born from love and feeling,
Neither have a voice,
Neither have a reason,
Neither have a choice.

Hatred fools the foolish,
Anger feeds the foul in life,
Fury fuels frustration,
Then chaos wields the knife.

Great rivers gather many streams,
As they flow to Mother Sea.
Each raindrop bears a balance,
Each has the right to 'be.'

The mingling of the raindrops,
Will wear down rock and stone.
If you can wear away your hatred,
You'll find love can stand-alone.

I THE BEHOLDER

I see sunshine skies and butterflies,
I see bees on bluebells bobbing,
I see silver streams, fishes in dreams,
I see humming birds, sweetness robbing.

I see woodland glades, forest shades,
I see deer and dormice dashing,
I see eagles soar, waterfalls pour,
I see sparrows in puddles splashing.

I see owls in flight, the wonders of night,
I see fox and stoat sly sneaking,
I see stars aglow; the moonbeams flow,
I see bright-eyes, at me, a-peeking.

I see rainbows bending, marvels unending,
I see children enjoying great fun,
I see a smiling face, in every place,
I see good deeds, always being done,

I see you think me a fool! I must never see cruel,
I see all things, with eyes that perceive,
I see beauty each day; I live life that way,
I see you could! If you'd only believe.

I see love know it's real, know its touch, know its feel,
I see open and honest and true,
I see the ugly in mind; I am not of that kind,
I see…! But…Why don't you?

NIGHT WALKS

Slowly... Sound slips
As sunlight sinks,
Shadow slinks,
Daylight noise tires of itself,
Makes room for subtler sounds.

Creaks and cracks,
A distant fox barks,
Moon time,
Snail trail light,
Silver sight.

Infinity speaks from a trillion star screen,
Bemusing me? Confusing me?
Hypnotised eyes scan endless night skies,
Eternity smiles across unfathomable miles,
A billion year old twinkle passes me by.

Moths stutter,
Hungry bats flutter,
Small mouse scuffles,
Silent wing swoops,
Dagger claw scoops.

Leaves listen; pass wind whispered secrets.
Vegetation voices I cannot hear, greenery gossip
beyond my ear.
Ceaseless din under foot, mystery message within
their root,
Fibrous fingers seek and find, earthly treasures
to which I'm blind.
Silently my spirit speaks.

Dust and space,
A different pace,
Heaven's heartbeat,
Sea and rock,
A different clock.

The moment within lasts forever.
Wind stilled, air chilled,
Visible breath hangs between life and death.
How thin the veils, as my mind sails,
I touch the timeless.

HOPE.

Still he stood,
Waiting,
Eyes constantly scanning,
Searching for happiness horizon.

BURNING

I reached out,
Received great pain,
Loves a furnace.
I'll reach out again.

WHO!

It's not what's in your life that is important.
It's WHO…!

WISE

Knowledge without wisdom,
Is a glass without water.

THE LOSER.

Who knew?

Who cared?

As he slipped away.

He felt,

He cared,

As he slipped away.

Broken in mind,

He was the sensitive kind.

Found the world fake,

It was too hard to take.

Up against the wall.

It's big and he is small.

Why don't they see?

Life's reality?

This is not some film your in,

Stop acting life…

BEGIN!!!

But the people turned away,

From the truth he had to say.

"Avoid that human pile"!

"It's rubbish with a smile"!

"Leave him he's just a boozer"!

"Another no good loser"!

So they left him lying there,

No one seemed to care.

The street like an empty hall,

Echoed his dying call.

"I love you!"

"I love you!"

"I love you all!"

Who knew?

Who cared?

As he slipped away.

He felt,

He loved.

Then - - -

He slipped away.

THE PROMISE

There is a promise in the sunshine
There is a promise in the rain
There is a pathway in a prism of light
It beckons once again

So many eyes are downcast
So many heads are low
So many miss the skyway sign
Never see which way to go

Wonder never lifts their dull sight
Wonder never fills their head
Wonder...? They leave to dreamers
Their dreams are a long time dead

If you look you'll see the archway
Coloured crossing to another land
Close your eyes and click your heels
Let joy lead you by the hand

God's promise is in that spectrum
A bond that's yours and mine
Walk with me over Rainbow Bridge
To that world where souls entwine

ENLIGHTENED

You are born from forever,
And you return to forever.
Always knowing the answer,
But too afraid to ask the question.

LIAISON WITH LIGHT

God walked with me today,
Didn't talk much.
Didn't need to.

WALKING WITH GOD

God made me cry today.
I remembered… he taught me to smile yesterday

WALKING WITH GOD II

God made me laugh 'til it hurt today.
He showed me how silly I am...

ANGEL PRAYER

Oh God…!
Let me sit with an Angel tonight,
Open my eyes to what's wrong and what's right.
Teach me true love; let me walk in light.
Oh God…!
Send me your Angel tonight.

Oh God…!
I sat with an Angel last night,
It opened my eyes to a beautiful sight,
It showed me love; it showed me light.
Oh God…!
Please send it to the world tonight.

HEART HEALING

Help heal my heart from hatred.
Seal my soul from selfish spite.
Let me learn life's only lesson.
Let all life in love unite.

FRIEND

This word is known by every nation.
Used in every language every day.
By every child and every adult.
But.... do they understand this word they say?

It means that you are cherished,
Trusted by others as someone true.
When in laughter or in tear times,
They know to turn to you.

It means should distance dim the detail.
Should time tease and test and try.
Miles nor years cannot undo,
This bond between you and I.

It means you give life value.
On your love one can depend.
Care, comfort and compassion.
Your priceless, you're my Friend.

GRATEFUL

Thank you for your smile today!

GRATEFUL (AGAIN)

Thank you for hurting at the same sight!

MAY

May my load be laughter laden,
May joys healing hand be mine.
May my cause be care and comfort,
May my reward be smiles sunshine.

THREE NAILS

I keep three nails to remind me,
Of a meaning, of a man, of a cross.
Of truth, love, light, and compassion,
Of mans blindness, hatred, and loss.

On that cross hung wisdom awakened,
Aware of mans anguish, and fear.
Knowledge is the nail that pains deepest,
Love always gives, what it holds, most dear.

So many years! ... Yet so few eyes have opened,
To enlighten one, was still worth the cost.
Caring is the nail that cuts cruellest.
In no darkness will this light be lost.

Mindless millions are still missing the meaning.
A sacred saviour is in all faiths, and all creeds.
Love is the nail that holds longest.
It's for you that this heart still bleeds.

Arise from your death sleep! ... Awaken!!!
Know in you, Gods light never fails.
The lie is the life you are leading.
Free your soul from your cross, and your nails.

ALL WAYS AND ALWAYS

Always look for beauty.
Always look for the ugly.
Always look for the wrong in right.
Always look for the right in wrong.
Always look!
Always look for the balance.
Always understand, then... understand you might not.
Always be honest with yourself and see your deceit.
Always be honest with others, they see it too.
Always accept.
Always hope.
Always attempt.
Always strive.
Always feel the pain, joy, delight, dismay,
                desire, disappointment,
                doom, dread, and wonder of life.
Always feel.
Always fear... Then... conquer it!
Always be afraid... of not being afraid.

Always be sure, but... never certain.

Always be ready… to be surprised... BOO!!!

Always be strong, by knowing your weakness.

Always be true, in your search for truth.

Always search beyond what you think you have found.

Always learn, first yourself.

Always love, beyond yourself.

Always dream, and then… make it real.

Always

BE!

Be all ways,

Search the ways.

There are many ways to the one way, yet…

There has always been 'THE WAY' to the one way.

LOVE AND LIGHT IS ALL WAYS AND ALWAYS

EPITAPH

Weep not for me now I am gone,
The restless mind must travel on.
Weep for yourself, the one you'll miss,
Send me your smile with your parting kiss.

Let no tears fall of deep regret.
The tears of joy run just as wet.
Let no mournful mood my memory mar,
Tonight I join the wishing star.

As lovers part for a lonely night,
Each craves the other while out of sight.
Yet in that craving are they not glad?
Of their time together, the joy they had?

Remember me in summer's sun,

My love of you, and of everyone.

I lived every breath, gave as much as I could.

I tried even harder when misunderstood.

I laughed every laugh, squeezed out every tear.

I lived so many lives, at least ten each year.

There was joy in my heart with every touch,

It's a joy for me to have touched so much.

It matters not how large or small,

It only matters that you recall.

I really strove each and every day

With my mouth, with my body, with my eyes to say:

"You were what made me, made my life worthwhile.

You were my heart, my reason to smile.

It was often hard, to my love to stay true,

But I'm so glad I knew love,

I'm so glad I knew you."

PROPHECIES

THE HORSEMAN COMETH

Horror how you haunt me

Revelations in my third eye

So few have heard the lie in life

So many breathe to die

Scrying all the stigma

Sacred signs fall into place

No fear, no care, - acceptance

Humanity lost its race

There's no bleak black oblivion

My face tilts to the light

Yet I know I must face extinction

What's beyond…it's beyond my sight

AWAKEN

Awaken! Aware! Arise from your sleep,
The pale rider approaches his appointment to keep.
Already the prophecy its purpose pursues,
Horsemen are riding your future they choose.
Fate is upon you through the folly of man,
Look not now for mercy, prepare as you can.
The seal has been broken, unguarded the gate,
The reaper is starving; his hunger is great.
Many messengers came, bore the word from above,
But greed governs and grips you,
hate rules here, not love.
Gluttons keep feeding while around the world crumbles,
As egos grow fat, truths temple tumbles.
Blind to the signs, the figures, the facts,
All knew what to do; even now no one acts.
Millions are dying, war, disease and despair,
As dummies decide on the right clothes to wear.
Nations are seething with disgust and disquiet,
Rage rampant runs, cities in riot.
This planet's been poisoned, plundered for profit,
The seas now a toilet, avarice won't get of it.
War, famine and plague slaughter all in their path,
Compassions unknown to the riders of wrath.
Are you deaf? Are you dumb? Unable to see?
All castes and all creeds hold the same prophecy.
It's not coming next year, next week or tomorrow,
It's already here! The age of great sorrow.
Are you blind can't you see?
Your soul knows it's coming,

To his tempo you dance, death does the drumming.
Foretold is this fate, there is nowhere to hide,
Only one place to turn to, that place lies inside.
In you lies the truth, the answer, the cause,
It's you who can save you, it's fate's hand you pause.
An endings been written, yet... within lies a choice,
Hark to your god self; hark to that voice.
The youngest of children understand what I say,
Know this voice as a guide,
in right and wrong everyday.
You learnt not to listen, lost compassion and care,
You must now face your guilt,
face your crimes if you dare.
Face the petty and pious; face the pride and the fear,
Face the cruelty you caused,
with your mocking and sneer.
Face the dark dwarf that controls you,
your cheating, your lies,
Face the cause for your hatred, it's you! You despise.
Cease your part in destruction; don't dwell in disgrace,
Cease following fools, it's God you must face.
Seven are the horsemen, seven times is the seal,
Seven are the plagues that nothing will heal.
This is not heavens anger; God gave you free will,
He steers not this sickness, it's human kind that does ill.
Those arrogant and ignorant in desperation drive on,
To what will they cling when everything's gone?
Take... keep on taking; heed not the cost,
Those without conscience, have nothing, they're lost!
Those empty vessels are marked with a sign,
The reaper will harvest all those he stamped 'Mine'!

No time is there left you, stand now or fall,
Those weighted by wrong won't stand at all.
Life leaves no blemish on the honest and plain,
No brand on the forehead of those who chose pain.
Mistakes? They made many
but their lessons they learned,
They awakened their soul sense,
by they're efforts they've earned.
There is no injustice, ever the choice was the same,
YOU! Made your choice, now you face the blame.
Armageddon or doomsday, of such people speak,
But the strong will survive,
there's much strength in the meek.
Purification, cleansing, of a world wailing with want,
Burning out blight in the darkness they haunt.
Time's trumpets will tremble;
shake this world to its core,
Of those dark days ahead, I can speak of no more.
My message is given... this herald speaks true,
Yours is the choice now, it now rests with you.
Of hope I will speak now, of when chaos is calm,
Light will bring healing, love is the balm.
All who remain in wonder will walk,
The key will be given, the doors will unlock.
On earth heavens kingdom will come as was willed,
We will walk with God...
The Prophecy...? Will be fulfilled!

About The Author
Richard Reid Ritchie

Richard Ritchie is a seeker of truth in areas that may hold answers to the bigger questions mankind has consistently pondered over. His life experiences to date coupled with a sharp focus in observing the human condition, blend together with a gift for utilising words to produce the inspirational writings that you are about to read in this volume.

Richard has been motivated to study a number of topics including hermetic lore, cabbalistic writings, philosophy, quantum physics and many other fields of learning, scientific, esoteric, metaphysic and mystic. This was done in an effort to gain deeper understanding and to make sense of what is happening to the world and it's peoples at this particular point in history. Often working with and from a spiritual source, Richard is actively helping people who have problems in their lives of either an emotional or physical nature by giving talks by direct involvement through and via one-to-one counselling sessions. These activities span working with prison inmates to addressing theosophical societies but in every instance, help and advice are offered to all who ask. He is a qualified therapist and healer utilising his skill and knowledge of both the physical and spiritual in a complementary combination that empowers and assists others

His writing, challenges us to reflect on emotions, behaviour and views related to the human condition and offers an alternative insight into the psyche.

Love is the motivating force that drives him and a wish to alleviate pain and suffering wherever possible. This reflects the hurt and the enlightenment that followed as a result of his own life's experience.
Like myself you will find his words empowering.

Gordon Wallace

Marie Corelli

Marie Corelli.

Printed in the United Kingdom
by Lightning Source UK Ltd.
121786UK00001B/130-174/A

9 781905 886982